Saint Dymphna's Playbook

"In *Saint Dymphna's Playbook*, Hillary Leftwich offers both a terrible testimony of endured violence and an invocation of absolution. With a variety of compelling experimental forms, readers confront the ways in which violence and sexual assault shape our understanding of the world and of ourselves. This book is '*a small tree in a burnt clearing*' — an incantation and an unflinching account of what breaks us and how we navigate survival when '*vibrations of our past … can never be buried.*'"

—Joan Kwon Glass, author of *Daughter of Three Gone Kingdoms* and *Night Swim*

"Hillary Leftwich crafts passionate lines with precise musicality. There's so much beauty here, washing over the brutally violent content until it drowns, blurry images at the bottom of a perfectly blue and dazzling poolscape. A cautionary note to readers frames *Saint Dymphna's Playbook*, Leftwich's brilliant and unyielding prose poetry collection. Yet this collection defies the language and logic of warnings. These are poems that instill awe instead of fear, joy instead of horror, love instead of loss. The warnings are the events of the poems, but the poems are events unto themselves: gorgeous line after gorgeous line, prayers, divinations, characters whose voices rise and thrive above the white noise of patriarchal violence. *'Hey, summer storm. You'll never know what it's like to swallow an ocean and still be empty.'* This collection fills up and up, pregnant with talent, with the nerve and drive to tell and tell and tell: secrets, stories, truths. A stunning book."

—Carol Guess, author of *Infodemic* and *Sleep Tight Satellite*

"Hillary Leftwich's relentless sentences vibrate with the alchemical aura of incantation. Saint Dymphna's Playbook is part spell book, part survivor testimonial, part cultural condemnation, part clinical investigation, part lineated essay, unflinching in tone and propulsive in tempo: this is a video diary set to alphabetical text or the reverse. Throughout her many experiments in form, Leftwich's forensic attention never forgets the primacy of interiority and the body's commitment to carry even the unbearable."

—Chris Campanioni, author of *Death of Art, Windows 85,* and *Drift Net*

"Harrowing, lyrical, and deeply poignant, Hillary Leftwich's previous book Aura was one of my favorite books of 2022. Saint Dymphna's Playbook builds on some of the powerful memoir material contained within Aura, while simultaneously being an entirely new thing. Hybrid in origin, Saint Dymphna's Playbook utilizes poetry, text and image, and short and long essays. 'Good Girls' recounts Leftwich's work as a private investigator—which is both sad and tantalizingly interesting—and the book's title essay draws out how who we once were deeply impacts not just who we are now, but also history as a whole. The culminating effect of Saint Dymphna's Playbook is of an artist creating at the height of her powers. A must-read for anyone interested in memoir and the creative act."

—Jeff Alessandrelli, director of Fonograf Editions,
author of *And Yet* and *Fur Not Light*

"Like the unexpected beauty of a bruise blooming under skin, Hillary Leftwich's voice rises from blunt pain and fury, as evidence of both the trauma and healing of violence. *St. Dymphna's Playbook* is a cathartic scream, capturing the horror and power of life in a woman's body. Society may wield the freedom to violate, ravage, and wound us without consequence, but Leftwich shows that we can transform violence into something achingly beautiful, witnessed, and shared."

—Gogo Germaine, author of *Glory Guitars:*
Memoir of a '90s Teenage Punk Rock Grrrl

"*Saint Dymphna's Playbook* by Hillary Leftwich demands of the mind and body a profound, visceral response—physical, emotional, and spiritual. From the moment I read the line *'Me with my lamb mouth. Her with her wolf heart.'* I knew I was stepping into a deeply vulnerable, raw space. This is a place many women fiercely protect, often hidden behind walls built from shame, anger, guilt, and a sense of otherness due to our particular traumas, experiences, and creative ability, wanted or not dictated by our unique biology. These barriers speak to the shared weight of feminine experience and how our collective agency has been quietly stolen. Yet society urges us to remain silent, sweet, compliant—*'good girls'* as Leftwich so poignantly writes. In 'The Woman Beautiful,' she hauntingly reminds us: *'We dream of erasing ourselves in mist and mud.'* Leftwich's words slice through the epidermis, divide veins, and shatter bone, exposing the struggle and strength of being a woman in a world that often seeks to silence us. This book goes beyond written communication; it is an experience of birth, baptism, death, and resurrection."

—Brenda S. Tolian, author of *Bestial Mouths*
and *Blood Mountain*

"A volume of poems. A diagram of loss and trauma. A book of prayers. A compendium of incantations. Hillary Leftwich's *Saint Dymphna's Playbook* is all of these things and more. Each word is carefully chosen to call close the spirits that might heal the worst wounds that humanity can inflict. A breathtaking, beautifully fragmented hybrid work like no other."

—Alex DiFrancesco, author of *Breaking the Curse*
and *Transmutation: Stories*

Saint Dymphna's Playbook
Hillary Leftwich

LIMIT ZERO Publications
Portland, Oregon

This book is published by LIMIT ZERO Publications
www.LMTzero.com

Cover Design by Olivia M. Hammerman
Cover art by Megan Merchant, meganmerchant.wixsite.com/poet
Interior Design by Gigi Little

Published in the United States of America
ISBN 978-1-938753-51-0

† A prayer to St. Dymphna,
patron saint of those suffering mental illness †

*Good St. Dymphna, great wonderworker in every affliction
of mind and body, I humbly implore your powerful inter-
cession with Jesus through Mary, the Health of the Sick, in
my present need. St. Dymphna, martyr of purity, patroness
of those who suffer with nervous and mental afflictions,
beloved child of Jesus and Mary, pray to Them for me and
obtain my request.*

NOTE TO READERS*

This collection contains themes of suicide, sexual assault, and murder. Do take care of your heads and hearts. Please visit the Rape, Abuse & Incest National Network (RAINN) for more information.

When I wrote these words, I was seeking a resolution that doesn't exist. Our voices continue to be overlooked, picked apart, and ignored. Our bodies do not belong to us, and we have little power over how men decide to use and govern them. I wish I could say in the past that I had been braver. Confronted a rabid dog sent to tear me apart. I'm offering my words to you, reader.

Maybe this collection itself is a brave act. Consider this a prayer, a ritual. A secret spell. Our final eucharist. Understand this: It never mattered if my words found themselves in the world. It only matters to me who reads them.

This note was written on May 31st, 2022, 24 days before ROE v WADE was overturned by SCOTUS. The decision to overturn was leaked before the decision was made final, but I know I am not the only one when I say it still hit me just as hard as not knowing what was coming. Since then, a ten-year-old girl in Ohio who was raped and became pregnant had to leave the state to travel to Indiana, whose abortion law has not gone into effect yet, to get an abortion. There is not enough rage collectively in this world to describe how this feels. I can only hope that we come together and set the small fires necessary across our states to collectively burn the bonfire to destroy what is the colonizing patriarch of our government. And for those who will lose their lives because of this decision and their family and friends, I promise I will never stop fighting, even when it might seem there is nothing left to fight for.

This book is dedicated to all the women/women-identifying/ LGBTQ communities who have suffered at the hands of those we trusted and those who never had our good graces in their hearts. And to my mother, who is the strongest person I know.

How does it feel to be dead? I say.
You touch my knees with your blue fingers.
And when you open your mouth,
a ball of yellow light falls to the floor
and burns a hole through it.
Don't tell me, I say. I don't want to hear.

—Ai Ogawa, "Conversation"

Queen of Martyrs, let me join you in this sorrow, and obtain for me the grace to fight against temptation and sin at the cost of effort, suffering and even life. When my turn comes, grant me, Mother, by your Jesus' death and your sacrifice, the grace to die in His holy Grace—the grace of a happy death.

—"Prayer in Honor of the Fifth Sorrow of Mary"

To sew is to pray. Men don't understand this. They see the whole but they don't see the stitches. They don't see the speech of the creator in the work of the needle. We mend. We women turn things inside out and set things right. We salvage what we can of human garments and piece the rest into blankets. Sometimes our stitches stutter and slow. Only a woman's eyes can tell. Other times, the tension in the stitches might be too tight because of tears, but only we know what emotion went into the making. Only women can hear the prayer.

—Louise Erdrich, *Four Souls*

Contents

CUNT RHETORIC

In the 1970s, *Hustler* magazine published a picture of a woman's face with a pussy for a mouth. The text beneath the picture read:

> *"There are those who say that illogic is the native tongue of anything with tits ... It comes natural to many broads; just like rolling in shit is natural for dogs ... They speak not from the heart but from the gash, and chances are that at least once a month your chick will stop you dead in your tracks with a masterpiece of cunt rhetoric ... The one surefire way to stop those feminine lips from driving you crazy is to put something between them—like your cock, for instance."*

Cock: A male bird. A penis. Nonsense. A firing lever in a gun in order to be released by the trigger.

I'm seven years old and a boy who lives on my street is babysitting me. I tell him my grandpa won a Purple Heart in WWII and he tells me to go get it he wants to see it he doesn't believe me so I do and then he sticks it down his pants and tells me I won't get it back unless I reach down and get it and boy won't my mom be mad if I lose it so I do because I'm scared my mom will be mad at me and my small hands push down his pants and into his underwear and I felt something harden against my hands as I grabbed the metal heart and as I do he pulls his penis out.

He tells me to put my mouth on it or he'll tell my mom and grabs the back of my head and pushes my face down and he tells me, "*Ssshhh, shut up.*"

Purple Hearts are awarded to American soldiers that are injured by "an act of any hostile force." Purple Hearts are not given to those suffering from post-traumatic stress disorder. Purple Hearts are not given to seven-year-old girls protecting Purple Hearts against a hostile force.

When I was a little girl, my mother would kneel next to my bed and sing me songs about cowboys and horses caught in wildfires and I would close my eyes and listen to her voice, all the while wondering if the horses were dying. "Did the horses die, Mamma? Did they?" "*Ssshhh,*" she sang, "*ssshhh.*"

A man I had never met before approached me at a bar and invited me and my friends to a party so we went because the bar was closing and when we got to his apartment he cornered me in his kitchen and offered me a red plastic cup full of beer from his refrigerator and even poured it for me. I thought *how nice* and in hindsight I thought *how stupid of me* and then he whispered in my ear like an angry animal, "*Wanna have sex in the bathroom?*" Everything went black when my face met the floor and I woke up in a bathroom naked on the tile and he was forcing himself inside of me over and over again and when I thought he was finally done two of his friends entered the bathroom and locked the door behind them and the last thing I heard was, "*She's just a stupid cunt.*"

The etymology of the word "cunt" derives from Latin "cuneus" (wedge) or "gwen" which is the root of the word "queen."

> *Queen, female ruler of a state, woman, an honored woman.*

A rape kit is called "processing evidence." A medical examiner will collect evidence including pubic hair, semen, skin cells, and any other physical traces left on and inside a victim's body. The medical examiner told me to relax. The medical examiner told me she can't do what needs to be done if I don't relax. The medical examiner told me to stop talking.

I couldn't move for five days afterward because my body was bruised and swollen and my son didn't know what was wrong with me and I told him, "*Mommy fell down and hurt herself,*" and he believed me because he was only four years old and he brought me cookies and he brought me his stuffed animals to watch over me while I slept and I never wanted to wake up again but the monkey named Fred was giving me this look like *get your shit together* and I wanted my mamma to sing to me about cowboys and horses burning in wildfires.

Horse experts agree to never ever turn a horse loose during a wildfire. Horses in the wild will always react to fear by running. A horse will die within minutes if a barn catches on fire. A horse will break its own leg to try to escape.

The DA told the detective working my case there wasn't enough evidence to take my case to trial. The detective stared hard at me. The detective asked me if there was anything I wanted to say. I told him, *"Thank you for listening to me."* I told him, *"Thank you for believing me."*

It takes approximately two to three hours for a human body to be consumed by fire. What's left behind is a three- to four-pound (on average) pile of ash and fragments of bone. A fire will continue to burn through flesh and bone and ash even when it appears dead.

Tell me how you would run through a fire. Tell me about the sparks picking apart your clothes your skin your hair until there is nothing left. Tell me how you wouldn't hear any more *"ssshhhs"* and no one would be forcing your head down no one would be forcing themselves on you, in you. Tell me about the sound of your feet and how it would be the only noise as they crushed the rough buffalo grass pushing its way up from the earth until you turned around and saw that you had run for so long the fires had all burned into nothing and yet there you were

no longer running

standing still

watching the fires catch on fire from behind you.

LAMB MOUTH

The cold month is coming and we are all sick with God-brain. Strike the match, light the prayer candle, speak their names. Our ancestor altar allows for coffee and pound cake. There is solace being found alone. A small tree in a burnt clearing. My girlhood gone bad. My nightgown slid. Sap from the bark where the knife stuck. The red fabric thaws on crisp sheets. I never wanted this virus. Sick with honey and fevered lamentations. Me with my lamb mouth. Her with her wolf heart. Don't offer me a rose and call this *love*. This sanctity without blessing. I can taste the lamb blood on my lips. Red apples falling on orange leaves. Sweet, sweet. This is me stoking the fire. A sheep sacrificed in flames. Only comes clean when it burns.

WATCH THE BURN

Consider this: I grab your hand, placing palm up, scribbles in messy ink. "*No one can read this,*" you laugh. Exactly. But you remember oceans I've never seen, so I stand on tiptoes, tell you to stop smiling. Breaths apart. Think cold, frozen seas. Soft seagrass. And your eyes, all gloss and gold, search for some kind of landmark that points to your grief. But I remember super moons, cigarette smoke, zigzags. Look at me. Somewhere, a damsel's dress is dropping. And you love fancy French biscuits, denim and dogwood, whistles under city bridges, cold clementines. The romance of vintage plagues. This is a story of you and me, striking all our matches. Watch the burn. And I'll go anywhere with you. Just remember a place neither of us has been.

NO LIKELIHOOD OF CONVICTION

Offense # 1 1102-0 SEX ASLT – RAPE – COMPLETED

"COMPLETED":

1.   FINISH MAKING OR DOING

    "HE FINISHED INSIDE OF HER, THEN THREW
    THE CONDOM IN THE TRASH TO
    CONCEAL EVIDENCE."

    ENDED, CONCLUDED, COMPLETED, FINALIZED,
    ACCOMPLISHED, ACHIEVED,
    FULFILLED, DISCHARGED
    SETTLED, DONE, WRAPPED UP, SEWN UP,
    POLISHED OFF.

2.   **Weapon Type: PERSONAL WEAPONS (BODILY
    FORCE)**

    PHYSICAL FORCE OR THE THREAT OF FORCE
    THAT PLACES THE VICTIM IN FEAR
    OF INJURY OR FEAR OF THEIR LIFE. ANY AMOUNT
    OF FORCE, WHETHER PHYSICAL
    OR MENTAL, THAT IS USED TO OVERCOME A
    VICTIM'S RESISTANCE IS ENOUGH TO
    CONSTITUTE A SEXUAL ASSAULT.

The FBI's definition of rape as of January 6, 2012, is:
The penetration, no matter how slight, of the vagina or anus with any body part or object
or oral penetration by a sex organ of another person, without the consent of the victim.

Colorado Revised Statutes (2013) defines "Unlawful Sexual Behavior" as follows:
When one person knowingly inflicts sexual intrusion or penetration (sexual assault) or sexual contact (unlawful sexual contact) on another person who does not consent or cannot consent to such contact.
www.thebluebench.org

Related Person(s)

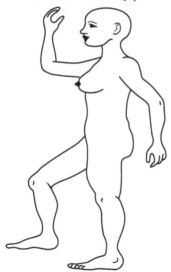

WHEN I TRY TO REMEMBER MY BEFORE-BODY, MY BEFORE-BODY REMEMBERS A MEMORY OF SUNLIGHT IN A PALE PINK BEDROOM FILLED WITH STRAWBERRY DOLLS AND DAISY PERFUME.

VICTIM # 1 –
CASE SPECIFIC INFORMATION:

The wisdom found in

the attempt to touch

is to feel the hard knot

of hurt and truth

while grief and blame: to know what is real and not
imagined
        not a memory based on another memory based on
        another.
        To know, despite the continual loop of flashing

Scenes   LIKE AN OLD MOVIE
Running   OFF ITS LOOP

EVERYTHING THAT HAPPENED IS THE TRUTH

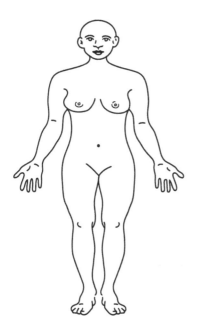

When I try to touch my before-body, my mind remembers what it was like to be a

human before I was tainted.

When I try to touch my before-body, my memory REMEMBERS a body that every human

has a right to carry.

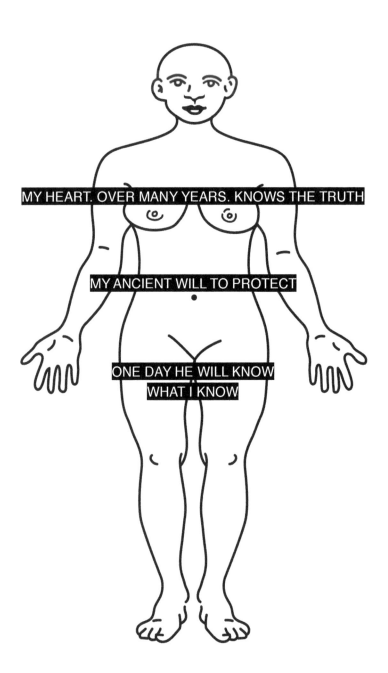

Someone once described trauma as carrying a body with you forever, unable to find a safe place to set it down. When my body was returned, it was listed as *without distress* and *well nourished*. My cavities were filled with the force of a thousand bolts of lightning.

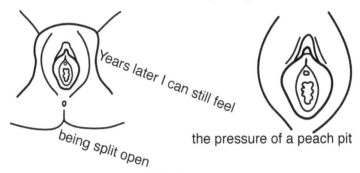

Years later I can still feel

being split open

the pressure of a peach pit

A pit torn out
Picked apart by anxious birds

I. *Tell my mother what no mother ever wants to hear but inevitably will (as a woman)*

When my body was returned

        it imagined itself as a girl

                not a woman

not a body

I can remember

HOROSCOPE

I've never seen you look like this. A season of freeze, rivers held in place. You stashed yourself down by the shorelines. "*So Sopranos,*" laughing. Nothing is funny anymore, and your body is thinning. You've pulled the root balls, trimmed, tucked away the grave of your heart. The ducks become small statues, wings forgetting air. "*I never saw it coming,*" you say. But you did. Your suitcase tied to a rope tied to your waist. Tethered to nothing. I gather my hair in knots, leave my shoelaces undone. Sometimes when I think you might brave the ice, I grab the rope, play captain of the seas, *pull, pull*. Don't believe what they say. Ice can hold a body for hours. But you know I'm lying, can smell the smoke on me. And I've broken the same ice, drowned in the same seas. Jagged glass on smooth seashells. A burnt sun sunk in tired windows. How to say: this is me, a hollow voice. A ghost left haunting your bed. Do you hear me? I am the thin red line, drawing myself, tethering the moon. I'll bear your weight. Don't believe what they say. Watch while the ice splinters under me.

YOUR BODY IS A BOMB

Open your eyes: Flash! Gimme grab-hands on your body. Laughter follows. It can't be this funny: laid out, bare as a buck skinned raw. He is tugging your innards out and shoving them in your face. "*Nice tits. You're a better fuck if you don't fight.*" The last song at the karaoke bar you sang was "Baby, It's Cold Outside," and boy is the irony settling in. He holds your heart in front of your face. You're surprised, because it isn't what you thought it would be. He is, too, because he hesitates, takes a bite anyway—tearing—his mouth a rabid dog. How is it? "*Tight*," he says. "*Just like your pussy.*"

Once, your daddy told you not to give your heart away to just anyone. But your body is a gown, heavy with bruised jewels adorning every inch, a bite-mark corsage blooming on your shoulder. He tosses your heart aside, and you watch as it rolls toward the locked bathroom door. Light shines between tile and frame, slicing across your face. An illumination of sticky tears and your whore's red lipstick cuts across puffy lips. Your hand is a fist holding clumps of your hair. You're a Joker now. A Stupid Girl. What do you call a bad lay? A waste of a roofie.

Open your eyes: There are facts to face, and you'd rather he choke you out now and hang your hide to dry. Sew together a purse or dreamcatcher for a gift. But your son is waiting for you, and the babysitter doesn't have a clue.

Your heart has been butchered and spat out. Maybe you can build a Lego heart, hang it inside your birdcage chest. Can mothers be hollow?

Your son is too young to know; hearts don't need a body to beat. The wolf has finished ravaging you and now he is bored, picking his teeth clean. The door opens, shuts. There you are, I see you. Your body is a bomb. *Get up*.

It isn't going to detonate itself.

A BODY TO BUTCHER

the deer remain hidden because they are meant to
be found   just bones now, no flesh

a plateau as a pin cushion
stuck
        rib cages
        and skulls

every year the abandoned trailhead, wrapped in ivy
tendrils
white tail   white spots   brown coat

simmers and stews from winter-weary stoves
bending with knives, we pluck the doe
from its gravestone of browning leaves

What has nature taught you?

be gentle when you cradle its velvet body
a girl-toy all our own   to pull serrated knife
across a body to butcher

snap bones
        crack muscles
        release blood beneath layers

Do all prey fight back?

we have histories of lying
on backbones   on knees   heads bowed
good girls, they tell us
north is a necktie   hung high   hung tight

Women
we know what's coming   do we question their
intentions?
while the dust sleeps
the forest settles
a necktie   a noose
pulled tight

all we ask
be gentle
          when you   find
            our burning bodies

we know what's coming   we know we will be found
when the old deer scatter

STILL MOVING AS IF IN SLOW MOTION

After the rape, everything is cold. Sterile cold. The kind of cold that sticks to the body for days, sometimes weeks. The condensation of shame and filth slides seamlessly down on the skin, always returning later, no matter how many hot showers.

Cold sticks to the body for days while the son is still young. Old enough to walk but too young to circle the block on his own. Still, it didn't stop him from sneaking out the back door one day wearing only a Howdy Doody cowboy hat and clip-on western belt. Two plastic guns in each holster on either hip, walking from the backyard to the front sidewalk, giving all the neighbors a show. Had the son turned left at the end of the block instead of right, he would have stumbled across the halfway house on the corner. The sagging window eyes of the two-story brick house were always open; the box fans inside each room blowing the salmon-pink and lemony-colored curtains out each window as a salutation—*Hello! Goodbye!* That's what the residents did, too. They never stayed for longer than a month.

Old enough to walk but too young to circle the block, the son knew where to go because the orange cat led him back home. The orange cat was named Pete, sometimes known as Pistol Pete, and all the neighbors loved him for his warm tummy he exposed when he rolled over on his back for rubs and deep tiger purrs. Pistol Pete led the son to the door, where the mother frantically searched the house. It doesn't take long to search the house because it's only 600 square feet and one level, other than the basement, where the washer and dryer sit. No one likes to go down in the basement of a 150-year-old tuberculosis house. The son tells the mother at night, as she's tucking him in under his Jurassic Park comforter, that the people in the basement cough very loudly at night and wake him up. He tells her with a serious look on his face, his eyes widening, and his lips pressed slightly. The mother goes down into the dirt basement, navigating the wooden steps carefully because she once fell, surprised she didn't break her neck. She felt hands underneath her and always wondered if the coughing people eased her fall. She didn't mind them. But they had to keep it down while they were sleeping, at least. That was the arrangement.

The cat Pete, sometimes known as Pistol Pete, sat before the basement door and howled. He knew the people below were cold, too, because they announced it. But the thick concrete walls absorbed their words, so the mother only heard them cough.

Because they announced it, the mother, the son, and the people who cough lived for a year together in the rowhouse and a year after the boyfriend moved out. The mother would leave thrift store tea saucers piled with Chips Ahoy cookies and sometimes a pocket rocket of Grey Goose at the bottom of the steps in the basement. The mother always fed everyone. Made sure they were nourished. The son liked the red Kool-Aid when he ate his mac and cheese. He preferred creamy cheese over the powdered.

The mother always fed everyone before the rape. She baked chicken in the tiny oven. The gas going into the oven only increased the temperature to 350 degrees, but if she kept it in long enough, it browned so that it came out sizzling in a butter bath. Discounted half-cakes from the grocery bakery. Sometimes red velvet, sometimes lemon custard. The mother liked buying half-cakes because the inside layers were exposed. A stack of sponge cake on top of a fiery-red filling.

Because the layers inside were exposed, the mother sometimes left a bag of groceries outside the halfway house. Cans of beans and condiments. The bread and butter pickles and palm-sized cans of sliced black olives sometimes scattered on top of pizzas. A man would peer down at her from one of the windows as the curtains tousled around his head from the wind. He made sure she left the pickles because those were his favorite. She had changed during the past few months. The first few weeks of June, she didn't drop off any foodstuffs. Then, just when he settled himself enough to trudge down to the corner liquor store and buy himself a jar of green olives, a bag showed up. He barely caught her leaving, but her body didn't travel the same. She moved as many of them moved amongst the walls of the house. He wondered how long she would stay.

The eyes of the son were always open. The body inside, cold and sterile. She knew her shame and filth fed everyone.

SUSPECT #1

Little did he know I had managed to escape from
the bathroom. Naked, crawling on my hands and
knees, I found my way to his bedroom window. He'd
covered it up with a Metallica fabric poster, but
I knew. Hands cupping the brown carpet, I made
my way to the window. As I passed his drum set,
my hand pushed down on a plastic deer toy, lying
with its head turned towards me, one eye staring,
unblinking.

Well?

Well, what? I found the window.

Take me with you.

*I can't. My hands. . . I stared at my hands
clutching the carpet. It hurt to move.*

Put me on your back, by your neck. I'll hold on.

*I did, and we crawled, the window so close now,
the silver Metallica logo meant to look like it
was made of lightning. But I was filled with more
electricity—I could feel every vein and muscle
moving inside me—a swarm of fire ants devouring
me from the inside. The fabric was thicker than
I thought and, as I pushed it back, revealing the
window behind it, I saw boards covering the glass,
a huge mountain symbol burned onto them stating,
"Big Bold Mountain Beer Taste!" and I knew.
I knew I wasn't escaping.*

SNATCH

I sing a song of sixpence, a pocket full of rye. Let me be a little girl again. Unaware of a bubble beyond sugar highs and Saturday morning cartoons. To know my mother and father are still married. To know my brother before addiction drowns him. Before the neighbor girl across the street wanted to play doctor, and I didn't. She called mine *snatch*[1]. Barbies posed, Barbie's face buried between the other Barbie's legs.

Four and twenty blackbirds baked in a pie. A man breaks into my bedroom and snatches[2] me. We'll live a life of danger and unlimited gas-station candy. The kind my mother refused to buy. I shoved Bottlecaps and Nerds inside my daisy-printed panties where no one would look. I hid other things, too. How, in the future, my kidnapper will kill me. We'll live in motel rooms, with a different bed every night. The highway will look softer at midnight than the crooked light of dawn. Warm donuts. Hot chocolate. A stuffed bunny named Fred from a souvenir shop in Lawrence, Kansas. My hair in man-made braids. Sloppy as the tufts of corn hair I pull from the cobs we steal. A million rows of corn, just for us. I make them into dolls and call them Betty and Frank. Everyone has a 1950s sitcom actor's name. *"If I can't have you, then no one ever*

---

1   Vagina
2   Snatch, meaning "A sudden grab."

will," my kidnapper will say, a sad, sagging sunflower in his hand. I will hand him Fred as a final gesture of my childhood disappearing.

When the pie was opened the birds began to sing. Me and my red plastic cup, poison blooming inside. He, with an easy leer and hard conversation. Wasting time, waiting for friends to arrive. Boom music and coughing laughter, my mouth wide as it angles toward the floor. When I wake up: Three men in the bathroom, me on the floor, exposed. He is smothering me; grabbing, pulling, pushing. His friends stand over us as they record on their phones, their *whoas!* and *get it!* bounces off the tile. The man on top of me is a shiny ad in *American Dream* magazine. The Boy Next Door with a power-play in his back pocket, ready to throw down. I watch myself outside of myself. I am sad spilled on tiled floor. A cliché of every rape joke thrown around late-night bar stools and broken pool tables. I will never find my way out of his bathroom. I will never find my way out of his bedroom and into a car that dumps me and my shame off on the corner of Corona Street and Downing. I will never find myself again.

Wasn't that a dainty dish to set before the king? Take me back to gas stations and motel rooms. To men who take me without asking. And I'll go. Because love is ciga-rette-smoke clouds and take-out dinners warming in Styrofoam squares. Fred in a bed and me writing on shower-steamed mirrors, *I know we are in love.* A delicate thing hiding from the light. Or maybe it's too dark today (and tomorrow) for lonely birds to ever sing again.

THE WOMAN BEAUTIFUL

Youth, health, and beauty are the three qualities sought by womankind. Perhaps in the triple quest, beauty stands first, but it is hard to think of beauty without roses and of roses without youth[3].

The first fault of the woman who is growing in years is the figure. It grows heavy and becomes the middle-aged figure. She sleeps a little longer in the morning; is a little more tired during the day; eats more than she used to; goes to bed earlier and is less careful of her appearance.

Woman: From Middle English womman, wimman, wifman, from Old English wīfmann ("woman", literally "female person"), a compound of wīf ("woman, female", whence English wife) + mann ("person, human being", whence English man); thus equivalent to wife + man.

Womankind has made the unanimous decision to withdraw from society.

We have reached a place where we no longer need the spare rib. This might seem strange at first, but the world

---

3   Prescott, Augusta. "The Woman Beautiful: A Treatise on How to Keep Young." *The Household Physician. A Book of Popular Information on Health and Disease*, Household Medical Co, Boston, 1905.

will get used to us being gone. Our bodies will transgress into collages of another time, another universe—tailgating on the light of dead stars—the outline for obituaries and orbitals, actual consequences begotten, a color unrecognized in an argument over grief and, *"Exactly what color should our grief look like, Ron DeSantis?"*

Female adults in general.
>   We dream of erasing ourselves in mist and mud.
"Woman is intuitive."
>   We dream of scratch-and-sniff sticker books.
A disrespectful form of address to a woman.
>   We dream the aliens return to take us out gently.
"Don't be daft, woman!"
>   We dream of walking the strenuous trailhead and
>   never coming back.
A female person who is paid to clean someone's house and carry out other domestic duties.
>   We dream of city carnivals and dangerous boys.
"A daily woman."
>   We dream of our bodies as the final Eucharist.
A person's wife, girlfriend, or female lover.
>   We dream of motels and mothballs.
"He wondered whether Billy had his woman with him."
>   We dream of church incense in sex rooms.

spouse suspect

significant other

feminazi

fiancée fractal

wife girl

nasty

lover missus

cat lady

hag

his indoors mistress

cougar

baby mama

patootie paramour

welfare queen

sweetheart girl

baby boo

nowhere girls

queen querida

mistress inamorata

twat

young lady

wife piece

trophy wife

lady consort

partner pussy

skintern

sister wife

DISPOSSESSED

At the women's homeless dinner, I mix shredded lettuce, apple slices, and ranch dressing into a bowl the size of the moon. Chicken bakes inside the industrial steel oven and potatoes steam on the countertop, waiting to be buttered. The women have chosen their beds. An older woman shakes her head when a younger girl claims the back cot was hers first. She tells the ceiling she's not getting kicked out when there are plenty of beds for everyone tonight. If the women are anxious, they don't let on. Tonight, it's about warm food and coffee with the brand-name powdered creamer. Oatmeal cookies and sugar wafers. Seconds of everything, no questions asked. Foot soaks and fingernail painting with a rainbow of nail polish colors to choose from.

I take a smoke break with one of the women out back in the alley. We talk about the moon and the forgotten people who scrape themselves down the streets, lost in their own thoughts. The night is busy with the laughter of the bars and nightclubs lining the blocks—sirens and screaming. Later, the women tuck themselves into bed, close to the edge of whatever form of contentment they have for the night. They are lined up in rows, swaddled under pink and purple fuzzy blankets—a nursery for adults. Claudia, the new volunteer who asks everyone for their astrological sign, calculates my suns and moons and tells me I'm as close to the Earth as anyone she's ever met.

As a girl, I remember being lost in a field of wildflowers, not caring if I ever found my way out. If I lived there forever, safe with the scents of columbines and wild bergamot. The cars outside on Broadway Street stop and go, stop and go, in rhythm with the bass music of the bars. The women settle down in their beds and make noises of contentment. Bellies full. Bodies warm. Outside the kitchen window, a man presses himself against the glass and points at the leftover food as I scrub dishes. He is a scarecrow, barely a man. His mouth opens and closes to the churn of the dishwasher. I look, but there is nothing left to give him. Scraps of chicken bones and potato skins. Remnants of salad with shreds of carrots. We are empty, all of us. I shake my head, but he doesn't see me. Someone in the back room taps out a sad melody on the piano, humming a familiar lullaby my mother sang to me when I was a girl. They tap and hum to the movement of the man's mouth, not caring that the keys are out of tune.

PAST HERTZ

I wake up every night unable to open my mouth. I'm grinding my teeth in my sleep. My dentist tells me it's either fear or stress. *Figure out which one or both, and you'll figure out where the pain is coming from.*

Pain can be a symptom of something hidden, waiting. A phantom group of cells. If you're in pain, try not to think about the baby kidnapped from your neighbor's trailer when you were twelve. You saw it on the news. Everyone did. The family dog shot and left to die. You were scared and tried to sleep in your mother's bed, but she pushed you away. You slept on the floor next to her bed, staring at her closet door. Your mother hid secret cardboard men in her, inside her, and in her closet. It scared you. Sometimes the hidden men turned out to be real.

The mandible is the only part of the skull consisting of bone able to move. Clenching your jaw while you sleep can cause overuse of muscles. Sensitivity to pain. It's a type of "hurt syndrome." Where the pain begins is unknown. Every pain has its root. Every pain must have an outlet, an ending. Everything is connected.

I've been feeling you in my bones. You're a low hum. You're the frozen field across from my house when I was seven. Seven was when I first realized I would die one day. Seven is the last time I was clean, untouched. In the field, no animal tracks scarred the snow. A perfect pasture.

The "Hum Phenomenon" stretched from New Mexico to the UK. Vibrations between 32 hertz and 80 hertz were reported. Once you hear it, you can never unhear it. The first time you were inside of me, I could never unfeel it, the static. I could never unfeel this feeling of static. This feeling is a frozen field. I want it to rest there, remain stationary, safe from itself.

When I was sixteen, our neighbor blew his brains out in his bathtub. The morning he died, I was touching myself under my fake satin sheets. The feel of the fabric against my legs was your skin, the feeling of your skin. More static. I heard the shot the second I climaxed, my knees buzzing. Later, the police said the suicide had been planned. Our neighbor woke up that morning and made himself breakfast. Eggs. Bacon. Hash browns. He climbed into his bathtub with his 9mm after writing a letter to his mother. His head exploded, his teeth scattering like pills on the blue bathroom tile. It took two days to find all of the pieces of his skull.

Suicide euphoria occurs after someone has fully committed to killing themselves. Happiness. Peace. Acceptance. These are all signs. Robin Williams was found hanging from a belt in his closet by his assistant. When going through his belongings, his wife discovered his watches were missing, and later found them in a sock, tucked away at a friend's house. When she asked the friend about the sock full of watches, they had no idea why Williams had hidden them there.

There are vibrations of our past that can never be buried. They said Williams looked like a cardboard cutout of a man when he was found dead inside his closet.

If we take away someone's euphoria, we'll never know where they hide their watches.

It took two days for the throbbing to stop in my jaw. It took two days for the hazmat cleaners to find the forgotten pieces of my neighbor's skull. It took two days for the family dog to drag itself from the abandoned field after it was shot, only to die alone on the doorstep, waiting for someone to return home. They never found the baby stolen from your neighbor's trailer.

I've been feeling static in my bones. Gun pop. Watches ticking. Frozen field cracks. You. Where pain begins is unknown. You're finding my forgotten pieces. They are hiding behind blood and bone. Untouched. Clean. Vibrating.

GOOD GIRLS

In my first few months working as a private investigator, I avoided high-profile murder cases until Rose's case came across my desk. Opening up her file, a stack of photos sat on top of a lengthy police report, and as I began to sort through them, I understood. This was the case that might break me.

The first photo, which corresponded with the coroner's report, indicated [Victim #1] splayed out on a slanted metal table while [Victim #2] is displayed on a tiny tray next to [Victim #1]. Rose's unborn baby's father isn't listed on the police report. The coroner for the county once told my boss that the dead like to keep their secrets safe. The blood from the autopsy condensing on the table looks fake, something you might see in a B-movie horror film. But it isn't fake. Neither are her hands, sliced from every angle. Defensive wounds, my boss tells me. He bites into a pink and orange frosted donut while we examine the crime scene photos spread across his desk. It's one of the first cases I'm assigned to as a private investigator that doesn't involve criminal mischief, assault, battery, stalking, or marijuana. It's my first murder case, and sure, all murder cases are bad, but this one went beyond anything I had seen on TV or in the movies.

I peer down at a picture of her face. Tangled dark hair sticks against maroon-stained skin. The coroner's report states dismemberment [see p.3 Evidence #10], and the body parts transferred into a green plastic storage container [see p.5 Evidence #12]. My boss cracks a joke, and I leave the room, the taste of acidic cold coffee bubbling up my throat. He later tells me in the break room I better start learning how to find a way to numb myself to the horrors of this job, or I won't last. You'll lose your mind. His eyes lock on me. He shoves half a tuna melt on rye into his mouth, chewing loudly. A scene from the movie *Benny & Joon* surfaces to my mind, the part where Joon is having a mental breakdown on a bus in the middle of rush hour traffic. She's pacing up and down the aisle, hands chopping the air, screaming. Later, I stifle my sobs in the bathroom stall, but they break free, crashing, big as waves against the cold tile. A woman in the stall next to me asks if I need a tampon, if I'm okay, and I tell her no, and no.

At night, I scroll through the victim's Facebook profile. Rose. *Making poetry in motion*, the caption under her photo states. She's young, less than twenty, older than sixteen, and somewhere in between she met a man who wanted her for himself and no one else. I've had my share of stalking cases since I took the job, but never murder. The small office in Aurora, where I work, has a strong connection with many of Colorado's top criminal defense attorneys. The owner, Ted, is an ex-Texas prison warden alongside a previous Colorado State Patrol trooper, Richard, as his sidekick. Together, they took me on, shoving out the last woman in my new position who secretly took other cases on the side. I wasn't that bold, and they knew it. During my interview, Richard told me he could tell if I was lying just by my body language. I sat tense on a leather sofa that was too soft in the middle, feeling myself sinking in and repeatedly having to adjust myself. They offered me the job the next day.

Folks in the business will tell you there's always a case that breaks you, and they're right. I worked dozens of cases previously, learning the ins and outs as I continued to be tested, Richard acting as my mentor while Ted did more meetings and courtroom work.

Between Richard and me, we soon became a "pretty solid team," as Ted commented one morning. He'd decided to treat us to a Keurig coffee maker and a water cooler to make the appearance of our tiny '70s office more legit. Until this point, I'd made plenty of mistakes, big ones, and was in constant fear of losing my job after seeing how quickly they let the woman before me go. Once, Ted threw a CD with a client interview on it and told me to "trash it; it's a done deal," I hesitated. If anything, Richard had taught me nothing was ever a done deal, but I threw it away anyway, feeling the need to unclutter my desk from too many pieces of paper and sticky notes. The next day, Ted flew out of his office, demanding the CD back, that the trial had taken a turn, and he needed the interview, realizing there was an important piece of information overlooked. I froze in my seat, knowing the trash had already been emptied and taken away, considering jumping into the dumpster and clawing open all of the garbage bags inside until I found it as long as Ted would stop murder-staring at me. But it was too late. With a slam of his office door, my time was up. Richard approached my desk, a giant smirk on his clean-shaven face. *Learn your lesson?* My face was numb, my body a balloon floating far away. He patted me on my shoulder, laughing, always laughing. *It's okay. He'll figure it out. He doesn't need that interview; he can work around it; he's just a lazy piece of shit.* My hands trembling, I forced a smile back, feeling the fragile, thin line between panic and relief slowly fade.

Most of the people we help investigate for their attorneys are arrested on bullshit, added-on charges to make their case harder to dismiss, or they really were innocent. The racially-profiled woman charged with bank robbery facing a lifetime in federal prison, her boyfriend already locked up in connection with the crime. Over 48 hours of listening to police radio communications proved an incorrect license plate, transposed by one digit, and I caught it. I remember sitting her down, and the three of us, me, Richard, and Ted, told her the charges had been dropped, she was cleared. Moments like these were worth the other terrifying realities of the job, the things I couldn't unsee. I keep telling myself it's worth it. But the client who nearly beat to death an old man known as "Santa Claus" in a shower stall at the local YMCA couldn't be researched into innocence, no matter how many times I read through the police reports. The former marine stalked his ex-girlfriend and threatened to kill her via the Jimi Hendrix song, "Hey Joe," then turned his rage on me, saying he could stalk me at the office and follow me home. Do the same to me. The eight-year-old boy who hung himself in his closet, his parents arrested for growing marijuana plants over the legal limit, their son growing cold at the county coroner, unable to arrange a funeral for him. Interviewing male inmates at the Arapahoe County Detention Center alone, because if anything, Ted and Richard ensured I was treated as equal and fair as a man would be in my position. But they didn't recognize or want to acknowledge that I am a woman in a detention center filled with men. There is no fairness in what a male inmate can do while sitting across from me in a small room as I interview him alone, with only a panic button behind me and a camera overhead to save me. My body covered in neutral clothing to "lessen the temptation," Ted tells me, of arousing any thoughts in our male inmate clients. But I also know the boy I inter-viewed, barely eighteen, arrested for assault and battery and attempted murder, could crack my neck in less than five seconds.

Then there was Richard, my mentor, who I later found out was fired from his job as a state patrol officer after being caught pulling women over and blackmailing them, promising if they agreed to meet with him at a motel room would dismiss their charges. The officers who arrested him found a collection of BDSM sex toys in the trunk of his patrol car, and it was all over. Working for Ted was his last hope, a lifesaving opportunity. After his wife divorced him, he moved in with his mother and thought about putting a bullet in his brain. I think about how when-ever I accomplish something worthy of praise, Richard always calls me a good girl. *Good girl*, he says, careful not to touch me. But the implication was there. It's still there, resting, waiting to be placed gently in my lap. I should take a compliment and tuck it away with the other well-meaning words that don't offer anything but discomfort.

Rose was a good girl too. Her killer, a previous boyfriend, is arrested along with his mother, who helped her son dismember Rose's body and stuff her inside a storage container. He told detectives Rose had broken up with him after a month of dating and that she wanted nothing more to do with him. When she begged for her life and her unborn child's life, he couldn't contain his rage at the thought of her with another man's baby inside of her. That another man had touched her. I watch the interrogation tapes over and over, watching Rose's murderer as he leans back, arms crossed, a look of satis-faction on his face. But he isn't our client. His mother is. And as I watch her being questioned by detectives, I see a woman willing to do anything for her son, including making herself an accessory to murder. Including giving up her life for a man who would murder a woman out of jealousy and rage.

Rose rests in my mind as if she found her own space to occupy, tossing my other memories aside. She remains, a dying root refusing to be unearthed. *Don't let it bring you down*, Richard sing-songs to me, forcing a fake smile while he saunters past my desk. *It's only castles burning.* I ask myself every day, how long will I last? How long until something snaps, sending me over the edge?

At night, I dream of curling my body around Rose. I hold fast to her, both of us resisting the pull of the current. *Meeting someone new*, Rose's last Facebook post stated, her face glowing and hopeful. I work on her murderer's case nonstop for weeks. Scanning text threads, Facebook posts, interviews, the 911 call, cellphone tower pings. The final ping on Rose's cellphone near where she was last seen on her way to meet the someone new. She never made it. There was no way to call for help, no panic button for her to push. One minute she was walking down the street, and the next minute she vanished.

That's what happens to women. We vanish.

There's another scene in *Benny & Joon* that sticks with me, one where Joon goes mad and gives in to her own mind.

Richard and Ted decide to give me a break from the case when I start making simple mistakes. After they tell me I'm focusing more on Rose than our client. I can't unravel myself from the feeling of being an accessory to helping a murderer's mother get a lesser sentence or entirely dismissed. I call in sick one day, and the next, and the next. I can't stop thinking about the autopsy photos, the last post on her Facebook, her face, warm and expecting, looking something like hope.

In my dreams, Rose and her baby are alive. The moon swings back and forth, a pendulum on a rope, hypnotizing us. She whispers words to me while the sun rises and sets outside. Years pass. When I look at her, her eyes are two burned-out coals. I wake up screaming, knowing there is no going back. That it's always more than the one case that breaks you, it's the people who break you and the people who broke them. There is no justice. There can't be. The scales will always tip to one side, or the other will never balance. And Rose, making poetry in motion, I can hear her singing, *Don't let it bring you down. It's only castles burning.*

SORROW, BABY

Chicago is mahogany and cocky bartenders. Rich, heavy fabrics with dark pockets in alleyways. The bubble bath we sink into is a dip in the moon. Night activity filters up from the windows, another windy night. Go figure. *Too many souls with no place to go,* I tell him. *So, they crowd the air?* Nothing softened his words. His bluntness cut through spheres of iridescence, souring the smell of lavender. I straddle him, hoping the distraction will change his mood. He's older looking than he sees himself. A younger version hides under flames from the candles stacked on the tub's edge, sacrificial offerings. *Lou Reed,* he said. *That's who people say I look like.* He laughs, knowing it's true. I'm not in the mood for talking, but he is, cupping my breasts, the weight balanced in each hand as if he has a decision to make. *Women these days just don't understand,* he says, and I am not ready to be mansplained about being a woman while I'm preparing to ride this man. *Let's have a baby and name it What-If,* I tell him, but he isn't playing. Instead, I lean down and kiss the words out of him, absorbing whatever sorrow he's about to lean into. *Let's have a baby and name it Sorrow, Baby,* he says, pushing himself deeper, our breath moving mountains. The night before I flew out, he drank whiskey and sobbed into the phone, calling me another woman's name. And me, not seeing the warning lights waning, offering my heart: a red apple left on an empty windowsill. Even better: I still have his Sorrow Baby growing inside of me. It's the shape of a tree with no leaves. We move together, soft silk tearing oh-so slow.

Darling: Too late. What-If is already curling inside me, taking hold with two claws.

Darling: But the wind grows impatient, a mad bird flying blindly into the window with no sign of stopping.

General Offense Information: VICTIM # 1 - LEFTWICH, HILLARY ELIZABETH

Operational Status: REFUSED BY DA - NO LIKELIHOOD OF CONVICTION

(This means no physical evidence)

This means no confession

This means "What were you wearing?"

This means "How much did you drink?"

This means "Why did you put yourself in danger?"

Reported On JAN-10-2008 (THU.) 1022

Occurred Between JAN-06-2008 (SUN.) 0100 AND JAN-06-2008 (SUN.) 0800

Approved On JAN-25-2008 (FRI.)

Approved By P89028 – For the purpose of this body, we will call the

investigating officers "Detective #1"

Report Submitted P04109 – "Detective #2"

Address: Where my body stains the bathroom tiles Apartment ###

Municipality: DENVER

County: DENVER

District 1 Beat 123

FELONY

Misdemeanor Family Violence NO

Offense # 1 1102-0 SEX ASLT - RAPE - COMPLETED

"Completed":

1. Finish making or doing.

"He finished inside of her, then threw the condom in the trash to

conceal evidence."

ended, concluded, completed, finalized, accomplished, achieved,

fulfilled, discharged,

settled, done, wrapped up, sewn up, polished off

2. Make (something) whole or perfect.

"Now I am tainted and will never be made whole again."

Location: SUSPECT #1 RESIDENCE/HOME

The bathroom inside his apartment fit three grown men, one in the act

of assault, the other two recording with their phones.

Weapon Type: PERSONAL WEAPONS (BODILY FORCE)

Physical force or the threat of force that places the victim in fear of

injury or fear of their life. Any amount of force, whether physical or

mental, that is used to overcome a victim's resistance is enough to

constitute a sexual assault.

UNTIL IT ISN'T

Women are slowly shrinking one by one, almost unnoticeable at first, until it isn't. Men tell us it's the law of nature for women to shrink, *it will be okay*, but we don't think they know. And we never blamed them for their gaslighting, for their rough skin and hands on us, the long, lusty stares, or the shade of their shadows across our backs. We are too concerned with things like safety or being heard when we scream. So, we scream "FIRE!" We scream "ROBBERY!" so people will hear us. The men were wrong anyway. It isn't the law of nature—it's us clinging on to the final moment before we are nothing. Because we have places to go and people to be. And every morning, we look at our reflections and think we're almost gone.

It's almost unnoticeable at first, until it isn't.

SIREN

He calls her *lover* now, this woman. Hey, happiness. Hey, perfect pink hearts. Once, I fell in love with a summer storm. But the rain fell harder, and so did we. Before he was yours: Heated lips, our skin stuck together, honey between us. His breath heavy as this pain. Thunder in my heart, lightning in the sky (where the lakes pretend to be oceans). But you weren't in our picture when we walked, hands braided together, me in my tiny bikini and his eyes filming me. *Siren*, he called me, my hair whipping around us, a black tornado. We stripped each other down when dusk stole the sky. The park by the woods outside town. Hundreds of trees, damp and thick. Secluding ourselves in his car while he pushed the driver's seat back, while I climbed on top of him, making him mine. It became a game of *gimme your mouth* so we pushed and pulled, ripping the fabric of our bodies until we came undone. My body a lie as it covered him. Does he call you my name? Not like a lover but like the demon I am. Like the song I keep singing he refuses to hear.

Once, I hung myself in the sky for him. But you are the sun he sleeps with at night. Hey, sweetness and truth. Hey, summer storm. You'll never know what it's like to swallow an ocean and still be empty.

SCARECROW

Let's sell what we own and go. But you're still hung up on how this will ruin us. I have higher hopes, having waited out life for you. To see you stretch higher than the pines. I reach you on tiptoes. Cover your mouth when you say my name. In another world, I straddle your bike, hugging you to me as you pump for the both of us. But they say, if you leave, don't ever come back. Instead, I show you how to split the sky. Break bluebirds before promises. *Lover for life.* My dress a pool beneath me, hand on heart. *Tell me what to do.* But you have the rapture on your lips. Tarnished tongues speaking for you. And it will take a crucifixion for you to believe me. I watch as you walk, parting the milk-weed sea. I'm still standing as if you'll turn, never mind the crows closing in. I'm just another scarecrow. I'm just another scream wearing your name.

OLD STARS

Old stars, make me a mother again. I know you died, but I need something shinier than dimness and dying light-bulbs in motel rooms. The smell of our wounds stiffening in late dusk. Men who don't mind staring hard and slow. Dollar store lipstick soft as a baby's skin. Finger fucking in between shimmering cracks. Glow, baby. Glow. Baby.

Old stars, I know you died but make me a mother again. Let me see my baby's wounds open as the light dims in dusky motel rooms. Hard men don't stare slow. Give me just a crack of shimmer? Enough for the cartons of vodka and cigarettes freezing on babies in dollar stores. Lipstick flushing pink for the dead. A baby's skin stiffening against a mother who died light-years ago.

A HOUSE IS JUST ANOTHER BODY WITHOUT ITS GHOST

Stranger Danger pays you a visit, so junkie-toss the bathroom, find your hidden plan. A plastic pill bottle. A stale cigarette. It isn't easy, is it? The neighbors pay you no mind. You're all mannequins in the same cardboard houses. No one is going to live through this. The city smells of paper burning. Words never written. Before you leave, Stranger Danger calls "*Shotgun!*" so now you're stuck with him. The mountains never seemed so close, and you remember your father. How he stumbled across his mother's old farmhouse. But people were living there. And you thought, *They don't belong.* You thought, *A house is just another body without its ghost.* Stranger Danger insists on stopping to get snacks. You realize he's your high school swim teacher. The one who used to ogle you in your navy swimsuit. Your breasts covered by slick shine, nipples erect. The coldness of the water always made you gasp. He told you to dive deeper. "*No, deeper.*" You listened, never questioning. The same time you listened when he pushed your head down in his lap. You never wanted it. But the bottom of the pool is a sanctuary. The fins of sharks are only seen at the surface. There are dues to be paid, and your time is up. You stop for snacks because you never eat Cheetos anymore. Thick notes fall from the radio, drop nostalgia in your lap. You lick the orange from your fingers, remember playgrounds and cartoons. "*You knew that it would come to this someday,*" your swim teacher says, bogarting the Cheetos bag. You nod, half listening. You have no plan in mind. You only know the mountains can hide a body forever if you know where to look. You're no sucker. Find your spot. Lean into the trees, remember your lover's mouth. How perfect their lips looked forming your name. When they spoke truths but refused to listen. How once, you thought this perfection was love. But you are imperfect, and no one can fix you. There's nothing left to keep you in place.

Take a deep breath and hold it.

I SECRETLY LOVE NOT BEING ANYONE'S BABY

Tell me the story of how you wanted me. There never is a happy ending, so please don't stop. Understand when I talk about crossroads, how the spirits of the dead are pacing (pacing!), and it's time to go. There's a faraway whistle of a train. Where? It doesn't matter. The sewer treatment plant pumps my poison. The beat-up cemetery holds my ground. I'm doing nothing wrong except being with you. The radio is playing an old sad song, and I hate you more than I love you. You never call me baby, and I secretly love not being anyone's baby. Call me a dead girl instead. "*Dead girl*," you say, reaching to kiss me. But I am just another skeleton you stripped the meat of. Hung silent to dry in the windows of home. As we near the crossroads, the train is closer. I watch your hands squeezing air. "Too late," I laugh. Taunt you with my curves. And "I hate this life," I say, staring venom at you. Whistling, flashing lights, it's all kinds of drama. I roll my eyes and jump.

"*Dead girl*," you say.

CLIPPED

The birds live in my bedroom now. They build their nests in corners with strands of my hair and shreds of clothing. We are home. The red light attracts the ghosts of ladies of the night. They bump and howl, filling my empty bed. They tell me it's okay to let go.

The bartender pours a beer and tells me the ghosts will love me if I leave a shot of whiskey out at night. "*Think of your-self as Santa Claus for the vagabonds*," he says. So, I do. In the morning, the glass sits full and sad.

The birds are in the stairwell again. They carry pieces of plastic, string, and other treasures scavenged from the trashcans in the alley. They build their nests high between iron crevices and rusted red brick, a safe spot where no predators can reach. But we can. Reach. And we do. We are everywhere with our candy rings and stolen Valentine's cards. Tokens of found love.

They say to call, but the phone rings in and not out, a vacant scream. They sit with an empty whiskey glass, holding allegiance, a two-man band and an abandoned room. I am the loose plant hanging above my living room window, waiting. When I clip the ends of the dying leaves, they still darken and curl.

My lost treasures and broken bones act as my hangman's noose. The ghosts are birds tangled in trinkets, watching their nests being picked apart, waiting for the edges to catch on fire.

The birds live in my bedroom now. We unraveled the trinkets binding their nests, searched for all we had lost. Ghost ladies of the night watch as I hang myself from the ceiling beam, holding allegiance. Still, the birds wait for me, full and sad. They tell me it's okay to let go.

The sound of their empty bones breaking, the sound of the brown leaves burning.

IDEATION

suicide (n.)[4]

"deliberate killing of oneself," 1650s, from Modern Latin *suicidium* "suicide," from Latin *sui* "of oneself" (genitive of *se* "self"), from PIE **s(u)w-o-* "one's own," from root **s(w)e-* (see **idiom**) + *-cidium* "a killing," from *caedere* "to slay" (from PIE root ***kae-id-** "to strike").

Detached from one's own body, though the mind remains [screaming]. If a mind is separate from a body, it can make a choice without the body betraying it. A poetics of self-regulation when all we want is to take the ghost off repeat. This small thing is comprised of old shadows and mourning. Once, absence. Twice, a hole we cannot name.

Take the pill. Release the safety. Tie the noose. Walk the cold path. An intimacy so sacred we can feel the movements, hear the voices—but what exactly is death, we cannot say. We know it as *lover. Seductive. Sinful. Savior.*

---

4   "Suicide: Search Online Etymology Dictionary." *Etymology*, www.etymonline.com/search?q=suicide.

WHEN I COME BACK FROM THE DEAD

When I came back from the dead, I came back as a color. Brambleberry burgundy. The color of dollar store lip gloss and sour gummy bears. When I returned, no buses stopped for me at shadowed street corners. Security cameras lost me in empty aisles, where teenagers wearing each other's clothes pocketed vapes and lube. When I came back from the dead, I found myself in old motel rooms, the dank smells of sex and bruises hiding under sheets like lost children. The janky ice machine buzzes an old, faded tune, and the whiskey dead gather in the cool smell of humid cigarettes and night sweats. When I returned, no buses stopped for a color. I found myself an old, faded tune, wearing other people's clothes. Shadowed street corners—lost security cameras find me. When I come back from the dead, this is the place I return to again and again. The birth of a body that never unraveled.

SAINT DYMPHNA'S PLAYBOOK[5]

[For all of us who continue to endure mental illness]

Create in me a clean heart, O God, and renew a right spirit within me. (Psalm 51:10)

Pray for purity. For I have sought unclean hands to bless myself. Break my bread and make me whole. A breath and a body left to rest in the mouth of the unforgiven.

Pass the road to your house. Jump-climb your bedroom window, fold into arms not meant to hold. What was I searching for in you? A me-and-you pact surviving the end.

I want someone to carry my heart. Hold it brave as a bomb after the pin is pulled.

---

5   Saint Dymphna was a seventh-century Irish virgin martyr. She was 15 (in about 620) when she lost her life spurning the incestuous advances of her father who insisted on marrying her to replace her deceased mother. When she learned of his plan, she fled from Ireland to Gheel, Belgium, but he found her there and beheaded her when she would not cooperate with him. There have been many reports of St. Dymphna miraculously curing the mental, emotional, and neurological afflictions of pilgrims to her burial site in Gheel. Based on these miracles and the story of her martyrdom, she was canonized in 1247 and named patron saint of the mentally ill. Her patronage also extends to incest and rape victims and runaways. https://catholicsaintmedals.com/saints/st-dymphna/

Naked I came from my mother's womb, and naked I shall return. (Job 1:21)

Pray for grace. A return of days spent grounded in a cradle of pillows and tired cartoons. My mother, a fixed figure, hung yellow in a backdrop of kitchen light. Breakfast resting on pink paper party plates, untouched.

I am a chaste child. Jump-skip from bed to faded floor-boards. Monopoly games and bedtime books. My father, the hidden hero cape on his back, always ready to catch me. Happiness: a shelter shifting me into sleep.

You stretch out your hand against the wrath of my enemies, and your right hand delivers me. (Psalm 138:7)

Pray for hands that have never touched me. Blackmailed friendships for pleasure. First- time fingering in back hallway bedrooms. Lamb lights shadowed by baby blankets. The last of the summer fruit falls, breaks. One last swollen sorrow.

My first sleepover. Scared and eager, anticipation of never-ending play. Friendship, a new manner of trust. Jealousy, a pink and purple nightgown. She let me wear hers, and we twirled in her basement, dreaming of boys we would never meet. Animals we would never see. And me, losing a piece of purity that became a bullet.

Whatever you ask in my name, this I will do. (John 14:13)

Pray for what you were meant to be and not for what you have become. A unicorn in a bathtub, turning. A horn pointed north. A steady gaze. The word *NO*. The feel of gentle hands on me, asking, *"Is this okay?"* A generation of curses forgiven. A gown of glass made just for me, impenetrable.

I could be you instead. You, not knowing the feel of fingers inside of you, forcing pleasure too young to understand. Blackouts and memories you own but hidden somewhere you can't find. I want my childhood back. I want the girl I should have been. Not me. Not this woman I am now, knowing the answer can be found in the pull of a trigger, so easy. So absolute.

The sacrifices of God are a broken spirit, a broken and contrite heart. (Psalm 51:17)

Bless my mind, for it knows not what it has done. Demons appear as angels in the light shade of dark. Holes punched in walls that were never there. I protect myself with rusted rosaries, believing they absolve. Each bead a tick of a heartbeat counting down to zero.

Grandmother's rosary beads hang on her picture. My ancestor altar exhibits generations of regret. Homesick heartbreak. Do they find in me what was once found in their own hearts? A tradition of suicide and sickness. The abhorrent alcoholic. Hear me, bloodline! What good are you if you can't save what needs to be cut from the flesh?

I call heaven and earth to witness against you today, that I have set before you life and death, blessing and curse. (Deuteronomy 30:19)

Bless my heart, for it once knew what I no longer believe. Carry this, as I once did the baby inside me, absorbing solitude, a burnt and broken shell. A memory of a soft sky. A rabid thing left weeping.

A baby, just for me. A savior. Love me forever. And I have never loved someone as much. A perfect person. And it's not fair to love someone more than you love yourself. And the room where you decided to keep him is old and may not exist anymore. The guilt of staying alive doesn't quite outweigh the desperation of an end.

For whoever loves his life loses it, and whoever hates his life in this world will keep it for eternal life. (John 12:25)

Bless your soul, for I forget the call of trumpets. The gun kept hidden, caressing the barrel in early mornings, a hardened lover waiting for my touch. The prescribed poison in pill form, the sturdy noose, waiting for the embrace of rope against neck.

I dream of possibilities. Of a savior sleeping next to me. I've come close to understanding the existence of a deity. He is a secret someone, tucked away. And the space between is the bloom of something beautiful. Abstained.

How long must I take counsel in my soul, and have sorrow in my heart all the day? How long shall my enemy be exalted over me? Consider and answer me, O Lord my God; light up my eyes, lest I sleep the sleep of death. (Psalm 13:2-3)

Bless your body, for I broke long ago, a bluebird crashing against my bedroom window. On the other side of glass, a live thing still moving. A lily pinned in place, a broken spine in my savage hands.

Pray for me, for this life, a useless prayer spoken in sacrament. And I am just a body, blessed and bruised, static and slipping, waiting for the devoted dead to return.

Only pretenders don't have a plan in place. And I am sad (all the time). Take away my fondness for forgiveness, and I'll find my way back to forgetting.

About the Author

Hillary Leftwich is a multimedia writer and the author of *Ghosts Are Just Strangers Who Know How to Knock* (Agape Editions, 2023) and *Aura* (Future Tense Books, 2022). She teaches writing at several universities, writing organizations, and nonprofits for adults, previously incarcerated and hospitalized youth, and unhoused populations. She centers her writing around themes of class struggle, the impact of disease, mental illness, ritual, and the supernatural. On the outskirts of the writing world, she teaches Tarot and Tarot Writing workshops focusing on strengthening divination abilities along with writing. She is a professional Tarot reader, death worker, and speaks with the dead.

Acknowledgments

"Good Girls" appeared in *SFWP Quarterly* (2022)

"Scarecrow" appeared in *Harbor Review* (2023)

"Saint Dymphna's Playbook" appeared in *Spirit: A Compendium of Esoteric Poetry* (White Stag, 2023)

"I Secretly Love Not Being Anyone's Baby" and "Siren" appeared in *Alice Says Go Fuck Yourself* (Agape Editions, 2022)

"Lamb Mouth" and "Watch the Burn" appeared in *The Night Heron Barks* (2021)

"Cunt Rhetoric" appeared in *The Rumpus* (2020)

"Past Hertz" appeared in *Big Other* (2020)

Also from LIMIT ZERO:

Box Girls by Aria Braswell
Against Common Sense by Brian S. Ellis
Predators Welcome by Dylan Krieger
Tuscaloosa Grief Factory by A.M. O'Malley